OTTERS

Published by Smart Apple Media
1980 Lookout Drive, North Mankato, MN 56003

Design and Production by The Design Lab/Kathy Petelinsek

Photographs by Joe McDonald, Mary Ann McDonald, Tom Stack & Associates
(Dominique Braud, W. Perry Conway, Ken Davis, Bill Everitt, Jeff Foott, Sharon Gerig,
Larry Lipsky, Randy Morse, Therisa Stack)

Library of Congress Cataloging-in-Publication Data
Whitledge, Jane.
Otters / Jane and Doran Whitledge.
p. cm. – (Northern trek)
ISBN 1-58340-071-0
1. Otters–Juvenile literature. [1. Otters.] I. Whitledge, Doran. II. Title. III. Series.

QL737.C25 W55   2001
599.769–dc21   00-050487

First Edition

2   4   6   8   9   7   5   3   1

NORTHERN TREK

OTTERS

WRITTEN BY JANE AND DORAN WHITLEDGE

SMART APPLE MEDIA

Underwater, in shades of blue and green, bright streaks of sunlight filter down from above. A slender shape glides into view. It has paws, teeth, and a tapering tail. Its dark body shimmers from the air trapped under its soft fur. Then it turns gracefully, curving its body to one side, slipping silently out of sight. This is the otter, an animal both admired and detested by people for centuries. Despite dramatic and destructive changes in its habitat, this amazing creature continues to survive all across North America.

OTTERS ARE PLAYFUL,

curious animals. They are also intelligent, being one of the few mammals that use tools. Some species use rocks to open the hard shells of **mollusks**. Around the world, there are 13 species of otters. Two of these live in North America: the sea otter (*Enhydra lutris*) and the North American river otter (*Lutra canadensis*). The sea otter inhabits only the West Coast of North America and its islands, while the river otter is widely spread across the continent.

The otter is related to the weasel, ferret, skunk, and wolverine. The North American river otter, in particular, has the long body typical of many weasels. Fully grown, it is from three and a half to four and a half feet (1–1.4 m) long and weighs 10 to 25 pounds (4.5–11 kg). The otter's dense brown fur appears shiny black when wet, similar to that of a seal, though these animals are not related.

An otter can have as many as one million hairs per square inch (6 cm²) of its body–25 times as many as a dog!

Otters are well **adapted** for swimming. A layer of insulating fat under their skins enables them to swim in frigid waters as far north as the arctic circle. They dive gracefully, their backs arching into the water, and vanish with a quick up-flip of their tails. These acrobatic feats are made possible by powerful, short legs and webbed feet that propel the otter quickly through the water. Its long, tapering tail acts as a rudder for sharp turns. The otter's broad, blunt head has small ears that help streamline it for swimming, and its whiskers help it detect food underwater.

Otters can travel underwater for a quarter of a mile (402 m) without coming up for air. While

Otters need to eat almost constantly to stay warm. They devour one-fourth of their body weight in food every day.

Overhunted in the 18th and 19th centuries, otters had virtually disappeared by 1911, when they were finally protected by international treaty. Otters were so rare that in the 1920s single skins sold for close to $2,500.

hunting, they swim very fast. Otters survive mainly on fish and **crustaceans**, which they usually eat in the water. If an otter catches a large fish, it will carry it to shore. There it will eat the fish, starting from the tail and using its powerful jaws and strong teeth to devour even the bony head.

Although they are mainly **aquatic predators**, otters may, on rare occasions, capture waterfowl

Otters have tough pads on the bottoms of their paws to help them grip prickly crustaceans and slippery fish.

Otters are the only marine mammals that eat, sleep, and carry their young while floating on their backs. Trapped air in the animals' thick underfur helps keep them afloat.

and small land animals. Their diet may also include turtles, frogs, and other **amphibians**, insects, and the roots of lilies and other water plants.

Strong-smelling droppings alongside lakes, rivers, and streams are a common sign that otters live nearby. These droppings are filled with crayfish shells and fish bones.

Tied as they are to the water, otters are surprisingly relaxed about taking to the land. It's not unusual for a group of otters to leave the water and travel into the forest, following a faint trail that leads to some distant pond.

The otter's short legs may seem ill-suited for land travel, but these creatures move quickly over land in a hump-backed lope. Even over deep snow, otters travel easily. They bound a couple of steps, then slide as far as they can, leaving a long, sliding track punctuated by footprints.

Otters are very social and typically live in small family groups. Males and females **breed** once a year. To prepare for the birth of her young, the female finds a hidden den near the water. This may be a vacant beaver tunnel or an enlarged muskrat den. Or she might use a hollow among boulders at the water's edge, or the space beneath the roots of a large shoreline tree. Where there are no trees or other cover, the mother pulls together grasses and other vegetation to form a shelter.

River otters have longer hind legs than sea otters. This helps them to move around more effectively on dry land.

In the spring, the female gives birth to one to five pups. The pups weigh about four and three-quarter ounces (134 g) at birth. They stay in or near the den until they're about a month old, and they can't see until they are about five weeks old, when their eyes start to open. The mother is attentive, sometimes carrying the pups on her back while they're learning to swim. Pups mature after about one year. Mother and pups groom each other and communicate in low, mumbling tones; a cough or grunt signals a warning of danger.

Otters actually help protect the kelp beds in which they live by eating sea urchins—spiny creatures that can overfeed on kelp.

River otters also communicate by scent. They keep track of each other through scent posts along the shore, where almost every passing otter leaves a deposit from its **anal glands**.

Otters are incredibly skilled hunters. Long ago, King James I of England kept a number of tame otters to catch fish for his table. He even appointed a "Keeper of the King's Otters" to tend them.

These scent posts are especially useful during mating season, when they help males and females locate one another.

The otter is fierce when threatened—it will fight rather than back down—so it has few natural enemies. However, because these animals reproduce at a low rate, they are especially **vulnerable** to disruptions in the environment. The North American river otter once inhabited almost all of North America above the Rio Grande, except for the western deserts. By the mid-1900s, though, it had been eliminated in many of those areas by damming, water pollution, shore development, and slaughter. Otter fur was highly valued. In addition, otters were considered pests that took game fish from lakes and rivers.

Today, through education and conservation, otters are admired rather than despised. They remain common in the Northwest, the upper Great Lakes region, New York, New England, along the Atlantic and Gulf coasts, and throughout Canada. Efforts have been made to reintroduce them into Pennsylvania, West Virginia, and several Midwestern states. But otters—and their habitat—need ongoing protection so that they can continue to enliven our waters and woods.

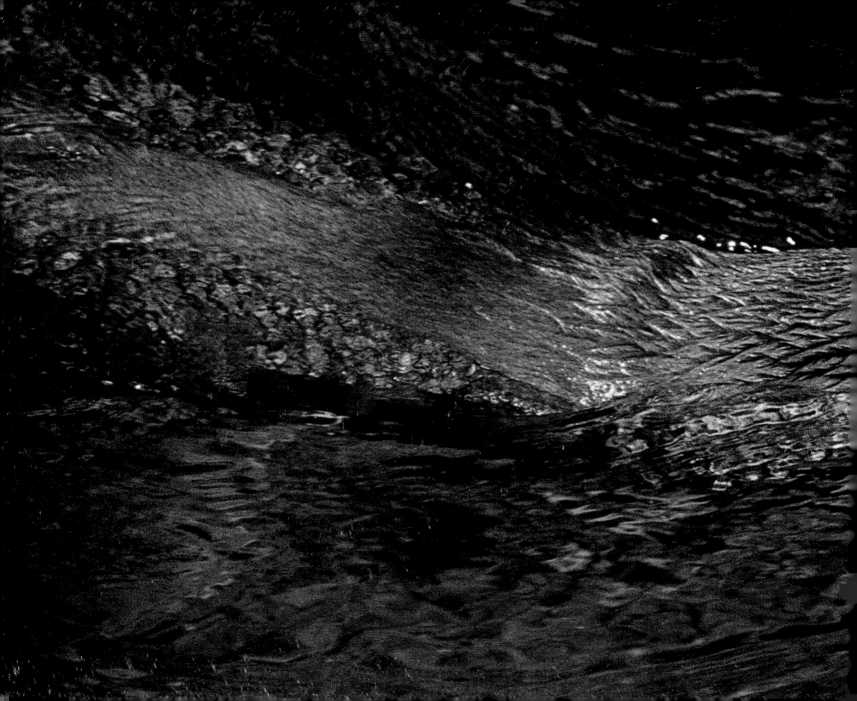

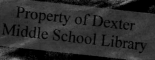

Otters have sensitive hearing and hold their ears upright when swimming. They listen for danger, as well as the movements of prey in the water.

RIVER OTTERS travel far and are not plentiful anywhere, so there is no place where they can be seen easily. However, anyone who watches for otters long enough in waters they are known to use will often be rewarded.

Although they are fierce when threatened by other animals, otters are generally shy animals and are likely to flee when approached by humans. Still, as you would on any trek into nature, remember that wild animals can be dangerous if approached. The best way to view wildlife is from a respectful—and safe—distance.

BOUNDARY WATERS CANOE AREA WILDERNESS IN MINNESOTA AND QUETICO PROVINCIAL PARK IN ONTARIO

These adjoining parks are set aside as wilderness, and most of their lakes and forests can be reached only by canoe. Together, they offer approximately three million acres (1.2 million h) to explore. The lakes in both the Boundary Waters and Quetico are excellent places to look for river otters.

ACE BASIN NATIONAL WILDLIFE REFUGE IN SOUTH CAROLINA

This sanctuary along the Atlantic coast has hardwood forests and both freshwater and saltwater marshes that harbor an abundance of wildlife, including river otters.

BAXTER STATE PARK IN MAINE

This park has 201,018 acres (81,412 h) of dense woods, steep mountains, ponds, lakes, and waterfalls. River otters are among the wide variety of wildlife at home in the park.

adapted: *adjusted to conditions*

amphibians: *smooth-skinned, cold-blooded animals that live part of their lives underwater, including frogs, toads, and salamanders*

anal glands: *glands at the base of the tail that produce a scented fluid*

aquatic: *taking place in or on the water*

breed: *when a male and female animal mate to produce offspring*

crustaceans: *soft-shelled water animals such as crayfish and crabs*

mollusks: *hard-shelled water animals such as clams and oysters*

predators: *animals that kill other animals for food*

vulnerable: *without defense*